A FOCUS ON...

ONLINE SAFETY

By

BookLife PUBLISHING

© 2023

BookLife Publishing Ltd.
King's Lynn, Norfolk
PE30 4LS, UK

ISBN: 978-1-80155-914-0

All rights reserved.
Printed in Poland.

Written by:
Steffi Cavell-Clarke

Edited by:
Kirsty Holmes

Designed by:
Gareth Liddington

A catalogue record for this book is available from the British Library.

All facts, statistics, web addresses and URLs in this book were verified as valid and accurate at time of writing. No responsibility for any changes to external websites or references can be accepted by either the author or publisher.

PHOTO CREDITS

Front Cover – wavebreakmedia, 2 – George Rudy, 4 – michaeljungm 5 – Dusan Petkovic, 6 – amophoto_au, 7 – Rawpixel.com, 8 – vystekimages, 9 – Oksana Kuzmina, 10 – mama_mia, 11 – CHALITSA HONGTONG, 12 – Kylie Walls, 13 – Dragon Images, 14 – Hilch, 15 – Olexandr Panchenko, 16 – Pressmaster, 17 – VTT Studio, 18 – Brian A Jackson, 19 – Alfira, 20 – Rob Marmion, 21 – Tomsickova Tatyana.

All images are courtesy of Shutterstock.com.
With thanks to Getty Images, Thinkstock Photo and iStockphoto.

ONLINE SAFETY

Page 4   Using a Computer
Page 6   Going Online
Page 8   Being Safe Online
Page 10 Security and Passwords
Page 12 Sharing Personal Information
Page 14 Using Social Media
Page 16 Making Friends Online
Page 18 Cyberbullying
Page 20 Asking for Help
Page 22 Top Tips for Online Safety
Page 24 Glossary and Index

Words that look like **this** can be found in the glossary on page 24.

Using a Computer

A computer is a type of **machine**. Computers are used all around the world and they can help you to do many different things.

Computers can help us do lots of things, such as drawing pictures, writing stories, playing music and learning new things. They are very useful.

"I love to watch videos on my tablet computer."

Ashley – aged 6

Going Online

Being 'online' means that you are using the internet. The internet is a **network** of lots and lots of computers that are connected to each other.

"I use the internet to speak to my friend who lives very far away."

Thomas – aged 5

You can use the internet on computers, tablets and smartphones. You might use it to play games or chat to friends.

Being Safe Online

Just like in real life, you need to make sure that you are safe when you are using the internet.

The most important thing you can do to stay safe online is to make sure that your parents or carers know that you are using the internet.

Security and Passwords

Passwords are words that you choose, and keep secret, to allow you to unlock a computer so you can use it. Passwords keep our computers **secure** and stop other people using them.

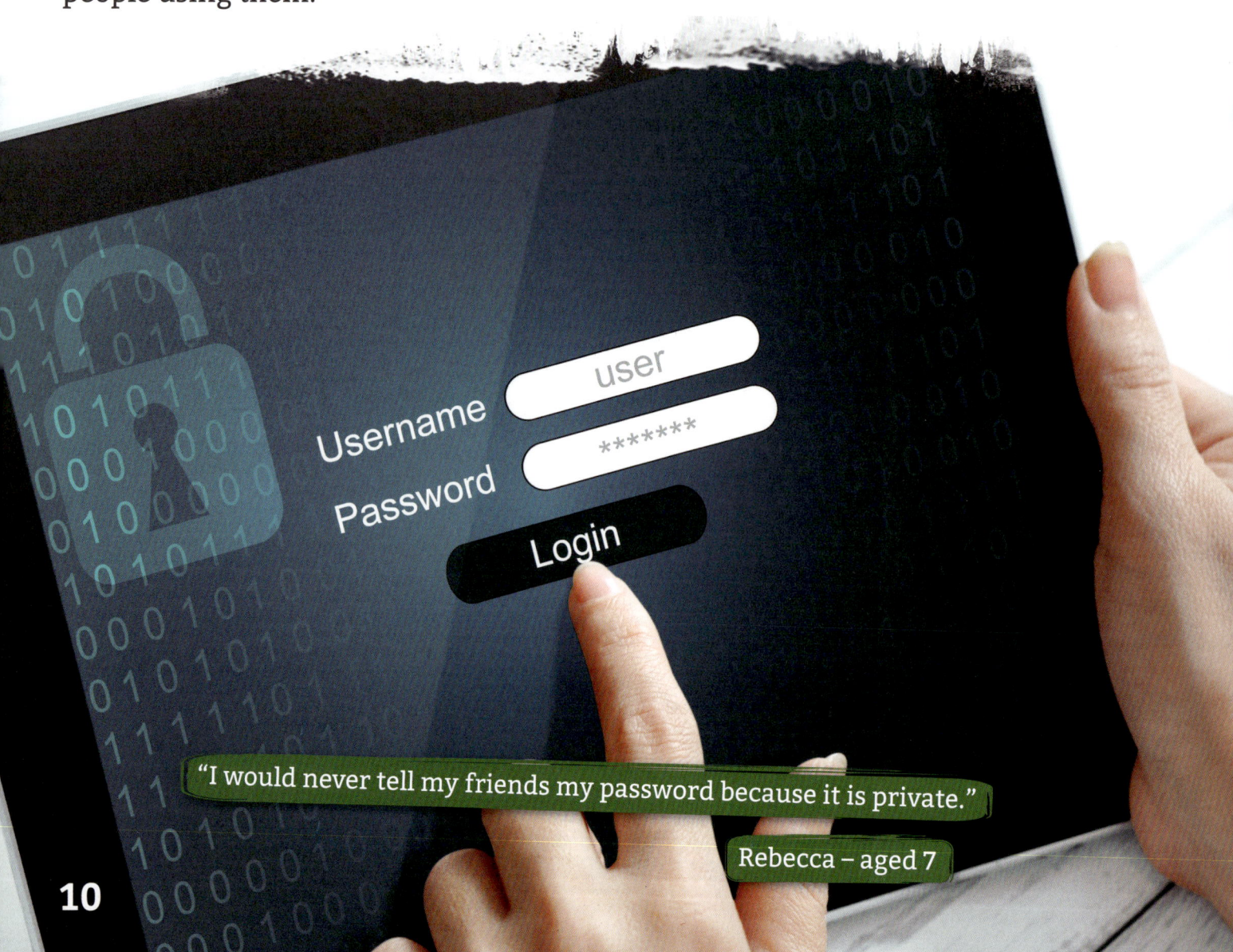

"I would never tell my friends my password because it is private."

Rebecca – aged 7

Try not to use things like the names of pets or friends for your password. You should use a mix of letters and numbers to make sure no one can guess what it is.

11

Sharing Personal Information

Personal information tells other people who you are and where to find you. Personal information includes your name, address, school and what you look like. You should not share this kind of information with people you do not know.

Never **post** anything on the internet that you wouldn't want the world to see. Once something is posted online, it may become impossible to remove.

Using Social Media

People use social media to **communicate** with other people from all around the world. Facebook, Twitter, Instagram and TikTok are all types of social media.

You can use social media to share information, photos and videos with your friends and family. Make sure that you keep your social media **accounts** private, so **strangers** cannot see what you are sharing.

Making Friends Online

The friendships you make online can seem very real, but they are not the same as the friendships you make in day-to-day life.

We usually cannot see who we are talking to over the internet. This means that it can be hard to tell if a person really is who they say they are.

"An online friend asked to meet up with me. I asked my dad if it was OK and he explained that I didn't really know who my friend was and that it might not be safe."   Richard – aged 8

Cyberbullying

Cyberbullying is where someone uses the internet to hurt, scare, or embarrass other people. Sharing private photos, posting nasty comments and sending hurtful messages are all examples of cyberbullying.

"My sister posted a photo of me I didn't like on Facebook. I told our mum and she told her to remove it."

Jessica – aged 6

People cyberbully because it's easier to be nasty to someone from behind a computer screen than in real life. All forms of bullying are unacceptable.

Asking for Help

If you see anything online that upsets you, or makes you feel that you are not safe, tell a grown-up who you can trust straight away.

Just like in the real world, people online can do or say things that upset you. Talk to a **responsible** adult who can help you be safe online.

Top Tips for Online Safety

Think before You Post

Don't upload or share anything you wouldn't want your parents, teachers or friends to see.

Think about New People

Remember that not everyone online can be trusted. Never meet up with online friends, unless you take a responsible adult with you.

Think before You Share

Never share your personal information, such as your address or telephone number, with people you don't know.

I always make sure that my parents or teachers know what I'm doing online. The internet is fun – but be safe!

GLOSSARY

accounts — the parts of a website that only you can access
communicate — pass information between two or more people
machine — a tool or device that can do a job
network — a system of connected people or things
post — upload something online
responsible — can be trusted to do the right thing
strangers — people you do not know
secure — safe

INDEX

bullying 18–19
computers 4–7, 10, 19
friends 7, 10–11, 15–17, 22
games 7

internet 6–9, 13, 17–18, 23
passwords 10–11
personal information 12, 22
posting 13, 18–19, 22

responsible 21–22
social media 14–15
sharing 12, 15, 18, 22
videos 5, 15

THE HEART

Alan Trussell-Cullen

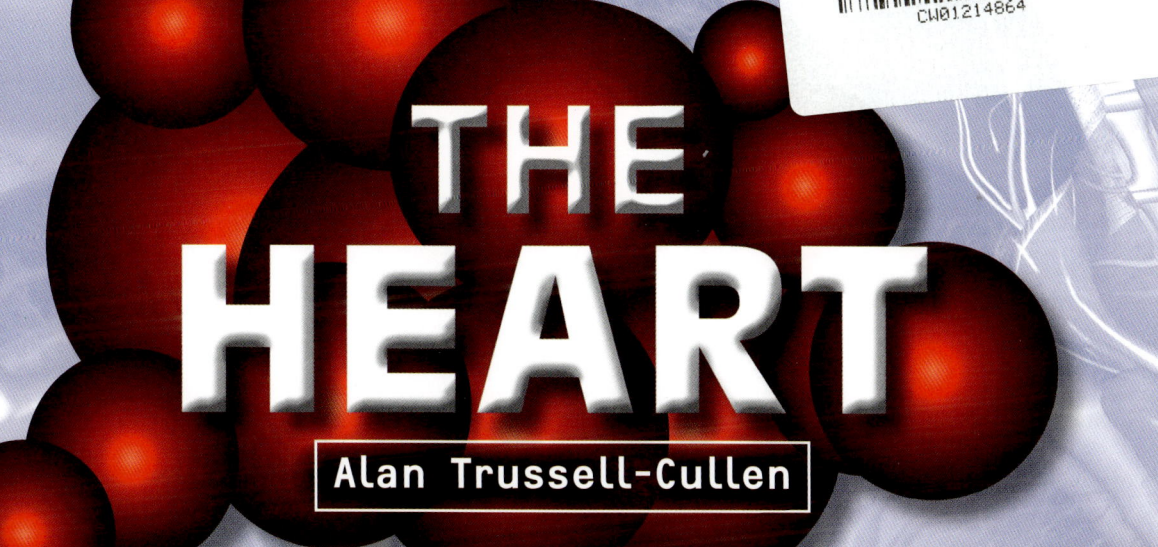

Nelson Thornes

Nelson Thornes

First published in 2007 by Cengage Learning Australia
www.cengage.com.au

This edition published in 2008 under the imprint of Nelson Thornes Ltd,
Delta Place, 27 Bath Road, Cheltenham, United Kingdom, GL53 7TH

10 9 8 7 6 5 4 3 2
11 10 09 08

Text © 2007 Alan Trussell-Cullen
Illustrations © 2007 Cengage Learning Australia Pty Ltd ABN 14058280149
(incorporated in Victoria)

The right of Alan Trussell-Cullen to be identified as author of this work has been asserted by him/her in accordance with the Copyright, Designs and Patents Act 1988

All rights reserved. No part of this publication may be reproduced or transmitted in any form or by any means, electronic or mechanical, including photocopy, recording or any information storage and retrieval system, without permission in writing from the publisher or under licence from the Copyright Licensing Agency Limited, of 90 Tottenham Court Road, London W1T 4LP.

Any person who commits any unauthorised act in relation to this publication may be liable to criminal prosecution and civil claims for damages.

The Heart
ISBN 978-1-4085-0106-1

Text by Alan Trussell-Cullen
Illustrations by Stuart Billington and Melissa Webb
Edited by Johanna Rohan
Designed by Vonda Pestana
Series Design by James Lowe
Production Controller Emma Hayes
Photo Research by Johanna Rohan/Gillian Cardinal
Audio recordings by Juliet Hill, Picture Start
Spoken by Matthew King and Abbe Holmes
Printed in China by 1010 Printing International Ltd

Website www.nelsonthornes.com

Acknowledgements
The author and publisher would like to acknowledge permission to reproduce material from the following sources:
Photographs by Getty Images/PhotoDisc, cover, pp. 12, 23/ 3D Clinic, pp. 4, 20 right/ Iconica, p. 5/ Stone, pp. 6 top, 18 right/ Taxi, pp. 7 top, 18 left/ The Image Bank, pp. 17, 21 top/ Asia Images, p. 20 left; Istockphoto, p. 7 bottom; Masterfile/Tim Kiusalaas, p. 21 bottom; Photolibrary.com/Foodpix, p. 10/ Photonica, p. 19.

THE HEART

Alan Trussell-Cullen

Contents

Chapter 1	**The Heart**	4
Chapter 2	**What the Heart Looks Like**	6
Chapter 3	**How the Heart Works**	10
Chapter 4	**The Beating Heart**	16
Chapter 5	**The Healthy Heart**	20
Glossary and Index		24

Chapter 1

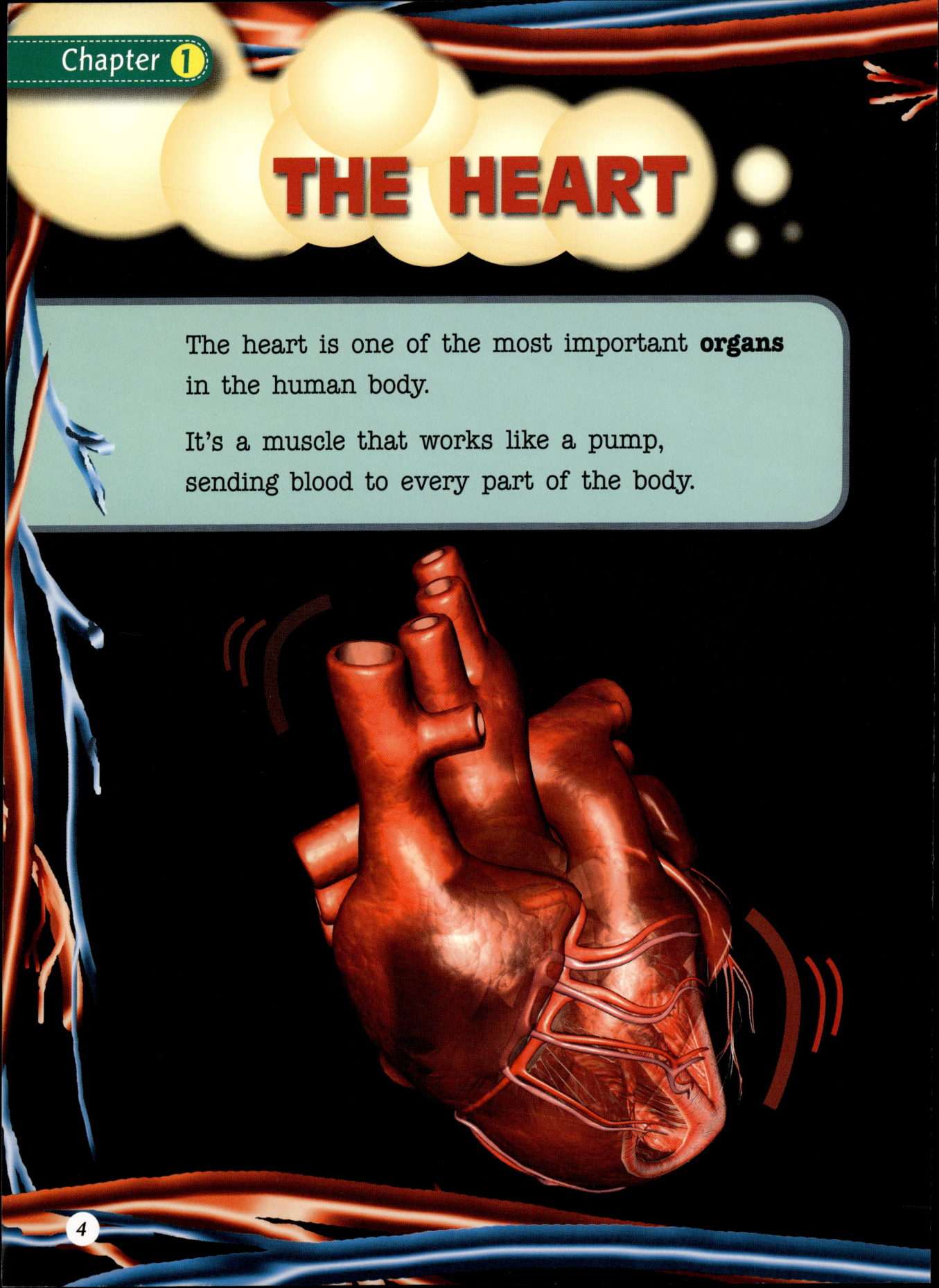

THE HEART

The heart is one of the most important **organs** in the human body.

It's a muscle that works like a pump, sending blood to every part of the body.

The body needs this blood to stay alive.

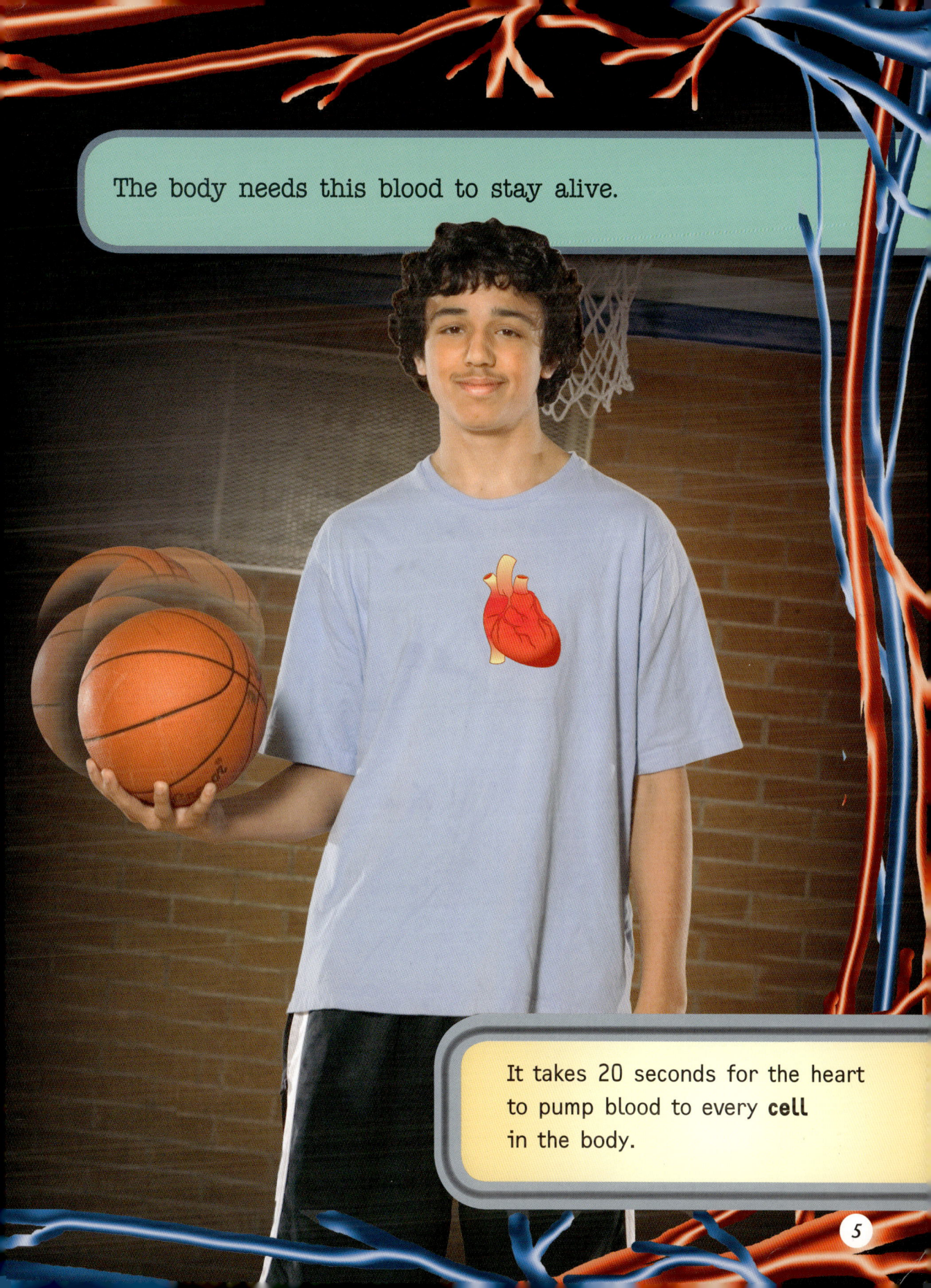

It takes 20 seconds for the heart to pump blood to every **cell** in the body.

Chapter 2

WHAT THE HEART LOOKS LIKE

The heart can be found in the middle of the chest, behind the ribs.
The ribs help to keep the heart safe.

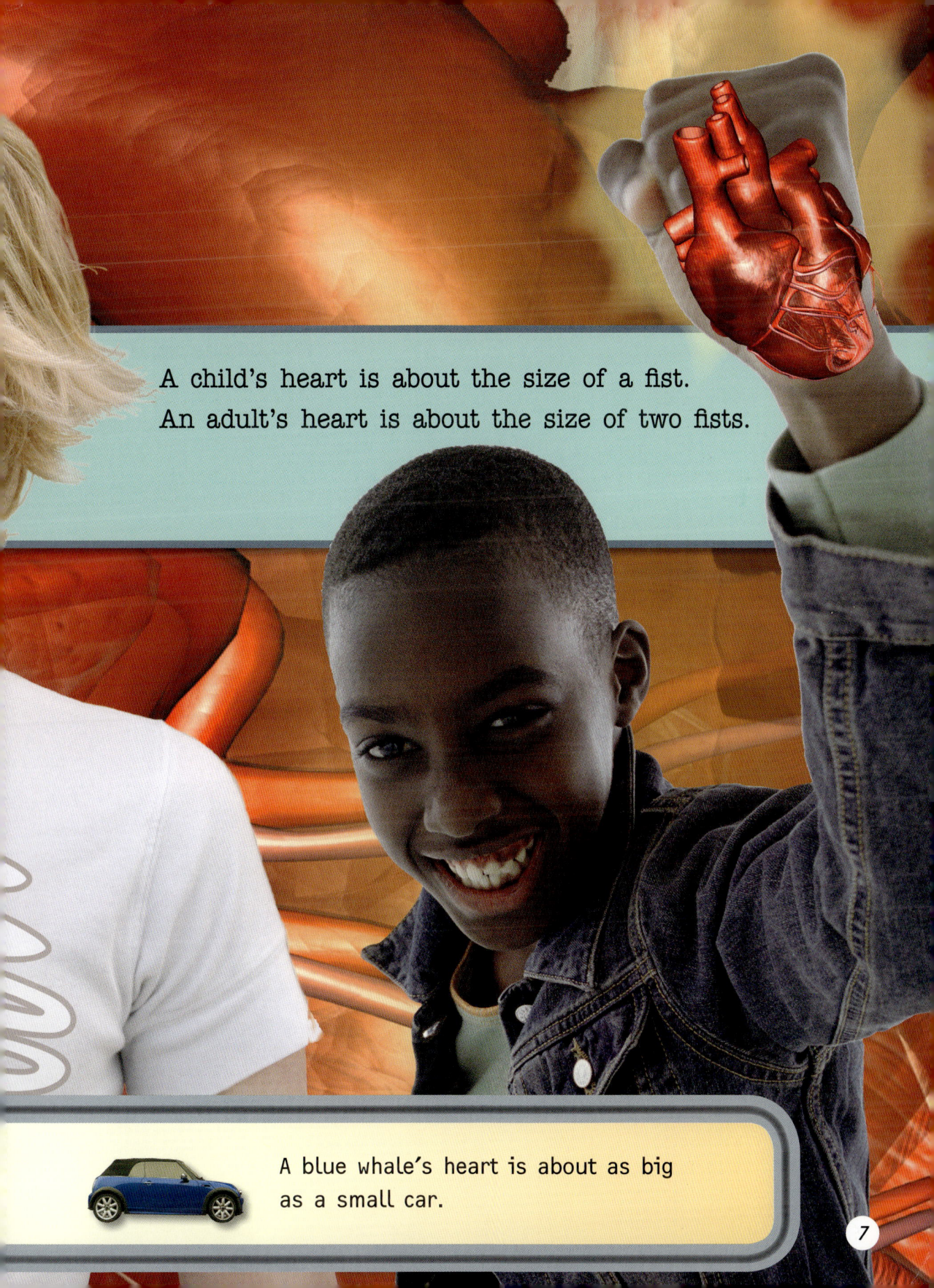

A child's heart is about the size of a fist.
An adult's heart is about the size of two fists.

A blue whale's heart is about as big as a small car.

The heart has four places that hold blood.

It has two large places on the bottom.
These are called the right ventricle and left ventricle.

It has two smaller places on the top.
These are called the right atrium and left atrium.

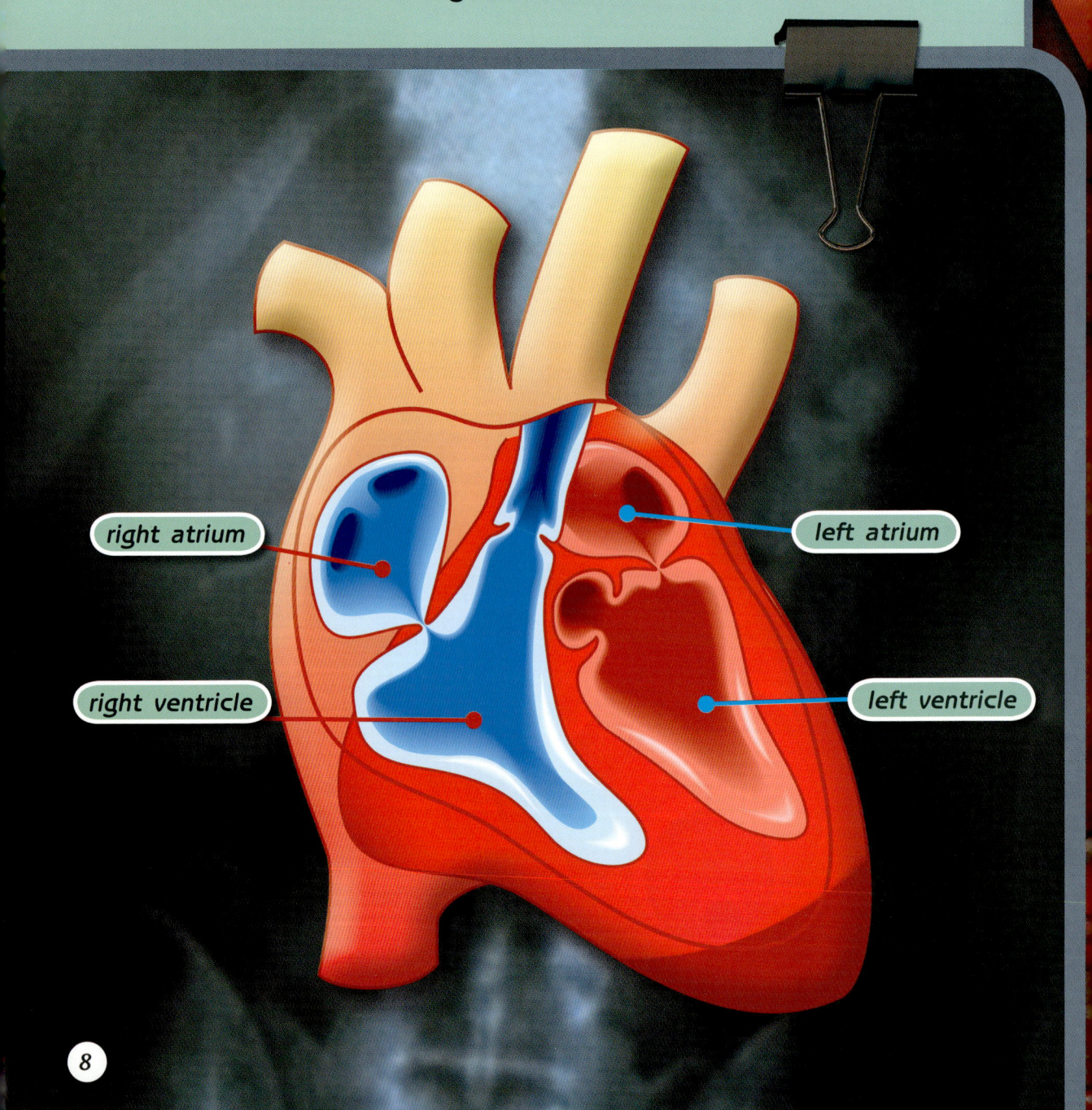

right atrium

left atrium

right ventricle

left ventricle

pulmonary valve

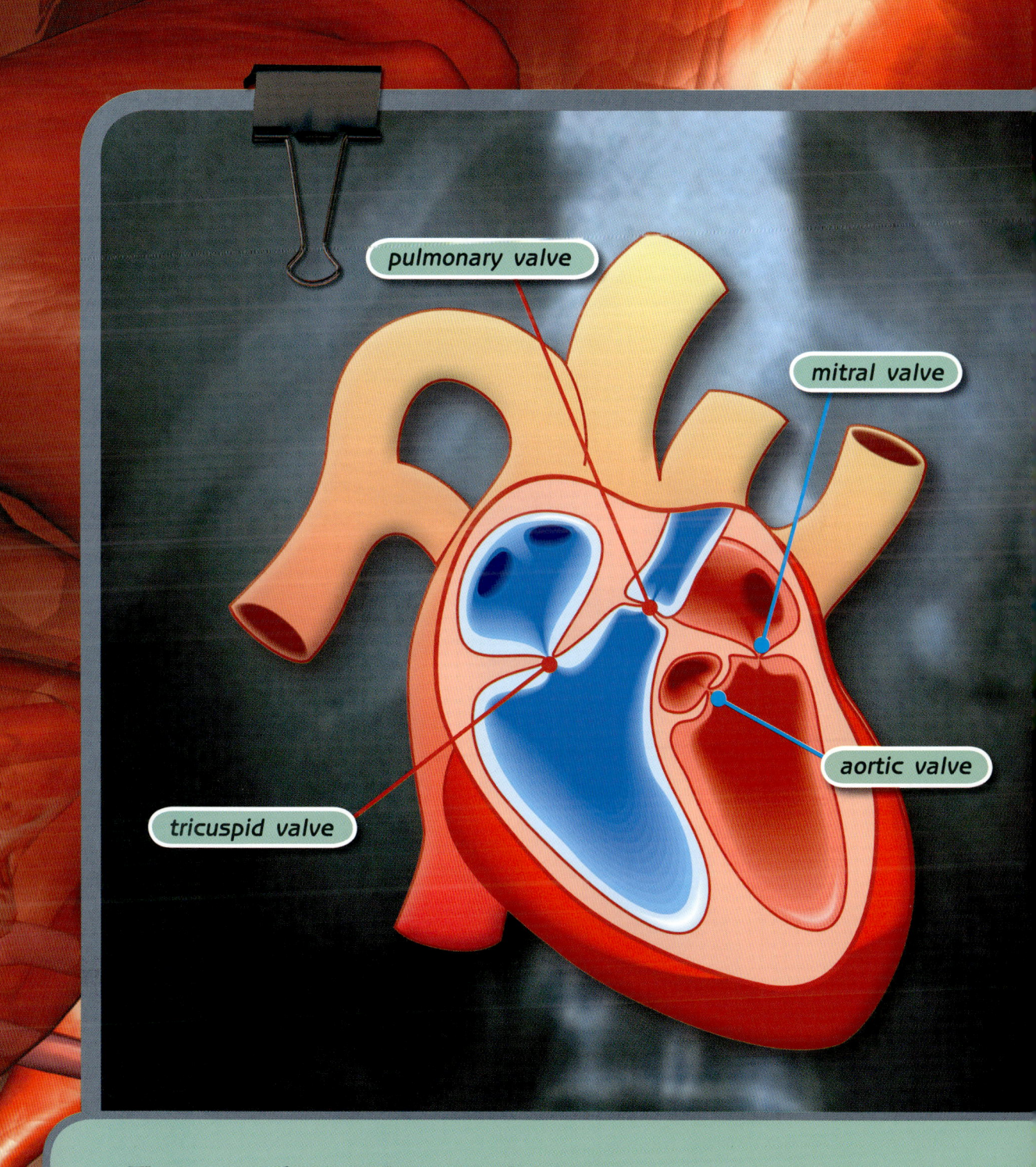

mitral valve

aortic valve

tricuspid valve

There are four **valves** in the heart.
The valves stop the blood going back the wrong way.

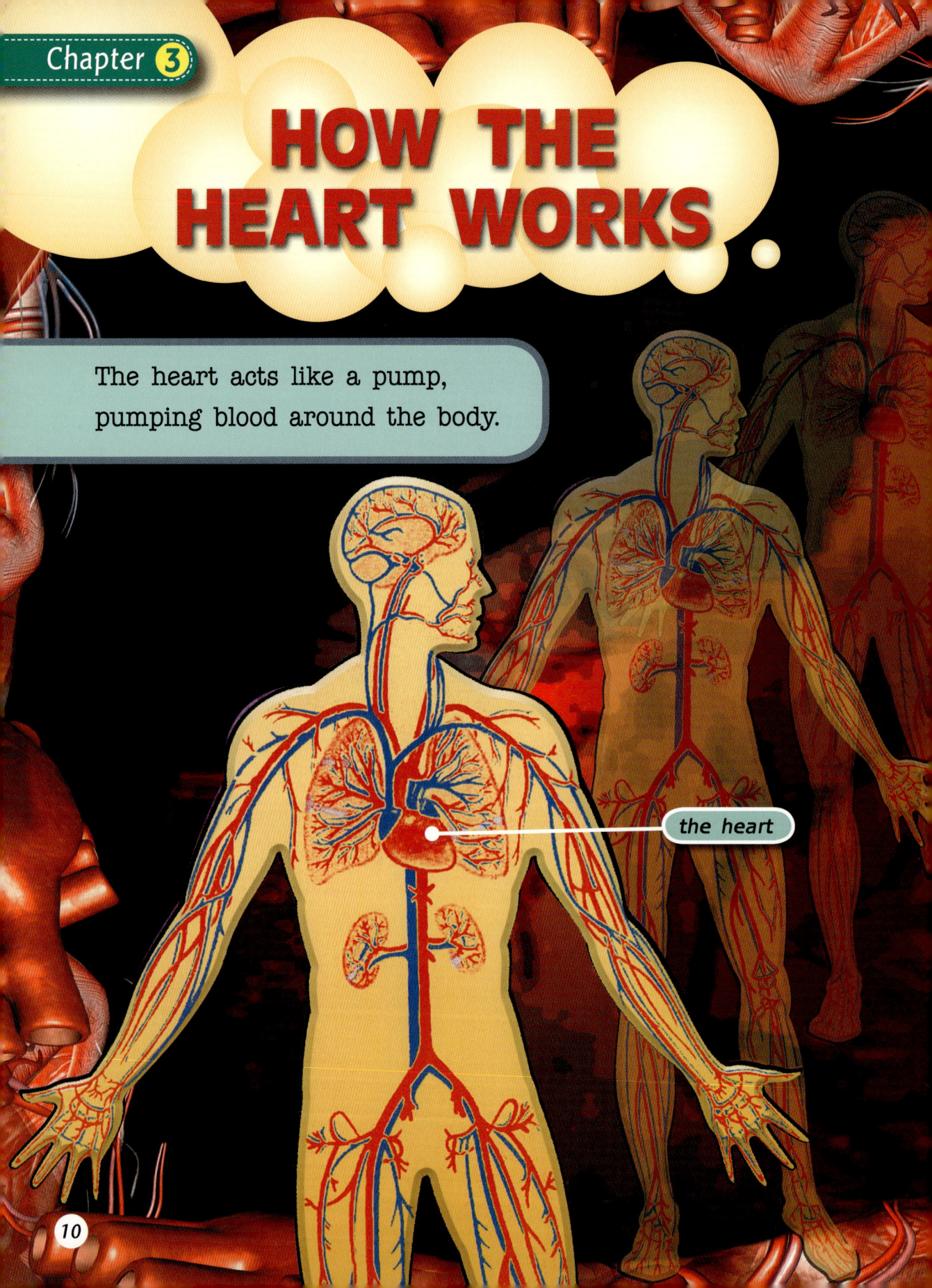

Chapter 3
HOW THE HEART WORKS

The heart acts like a pump, pumping blood around the body.

the heart

The blood takes important things like oxygen and food
to every part of the body.
Without oxygen and food,
the body's cells begin to die.
The blood also takes away things
the body doesn't need.

About 8 million blood cells die every second.
The same number of blood cells are born
every second.

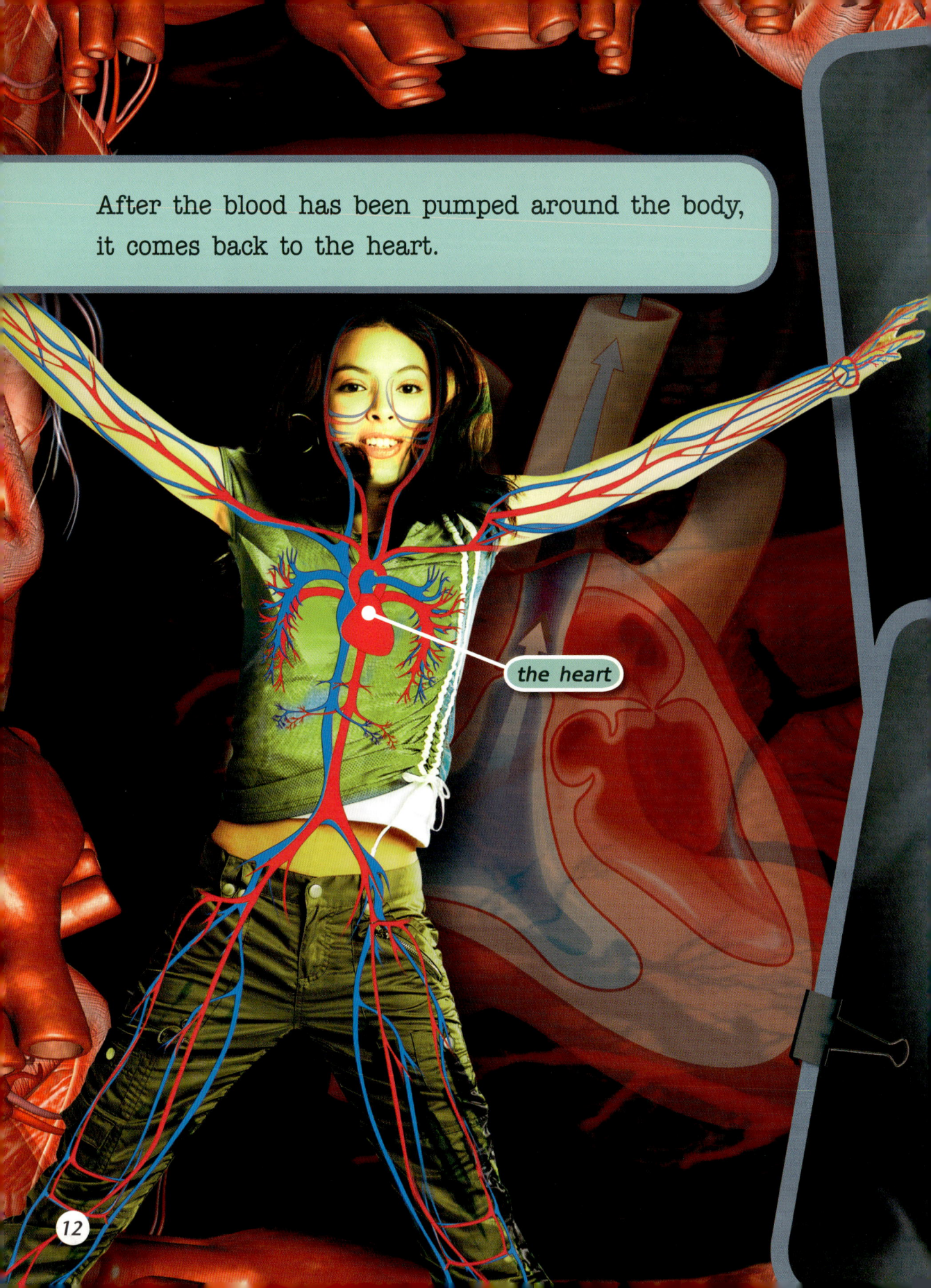

After the blood has been pumped around the body, it comes back to the heart.

the heart

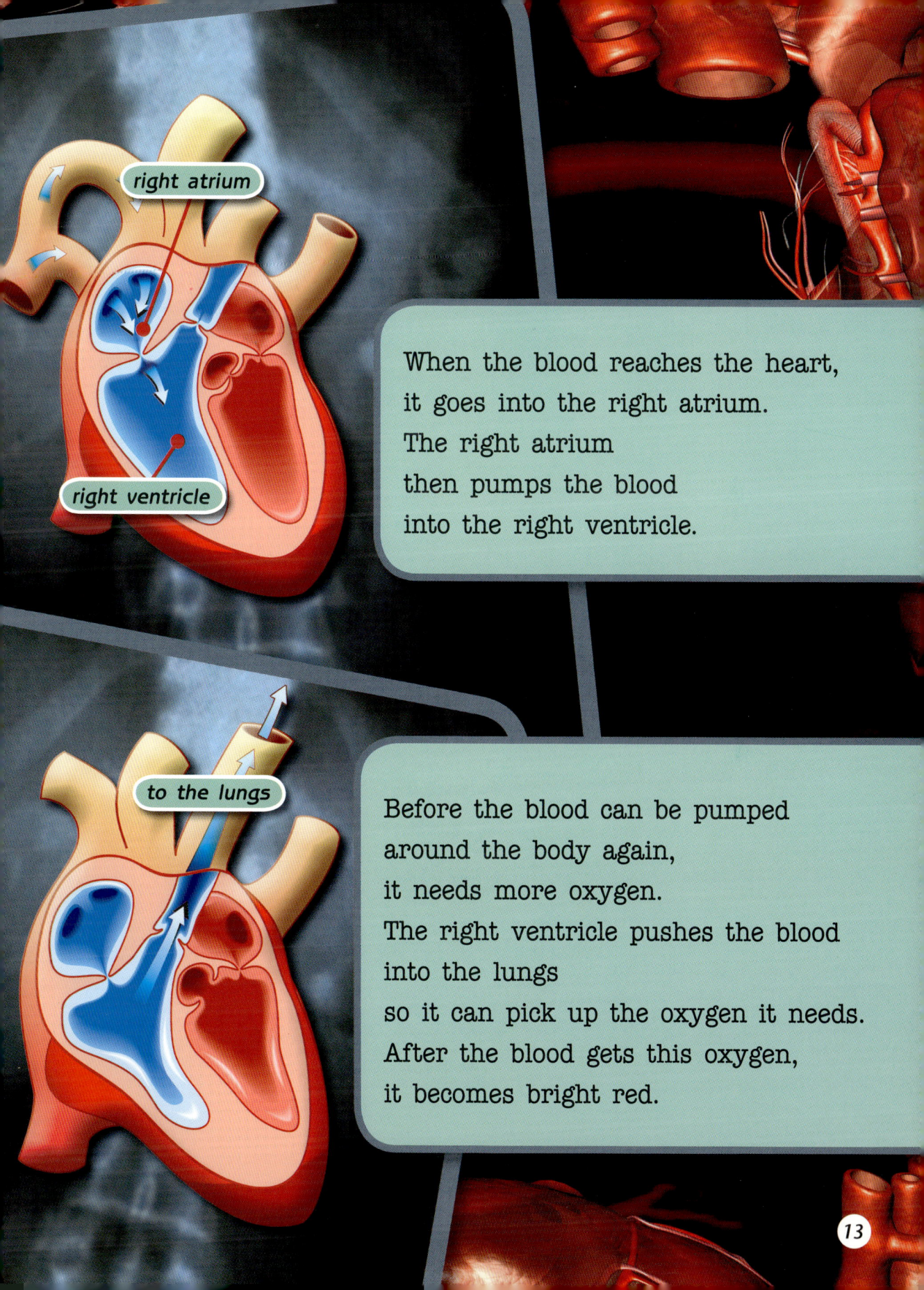

right atrium

right ventricle

When the blood reaches the heart,
it goes into the right atrium.
The right atrium
then pumps the blood
into the right ventricle.

to the lungs

Before the blood can be pumped
around the body again,
it needs more oxygen.
The right ventricle pushes the blood
into the lungs
so it can pick up the oxygen it needs.
After the blood gets this oxygen,
it becomes bright red.

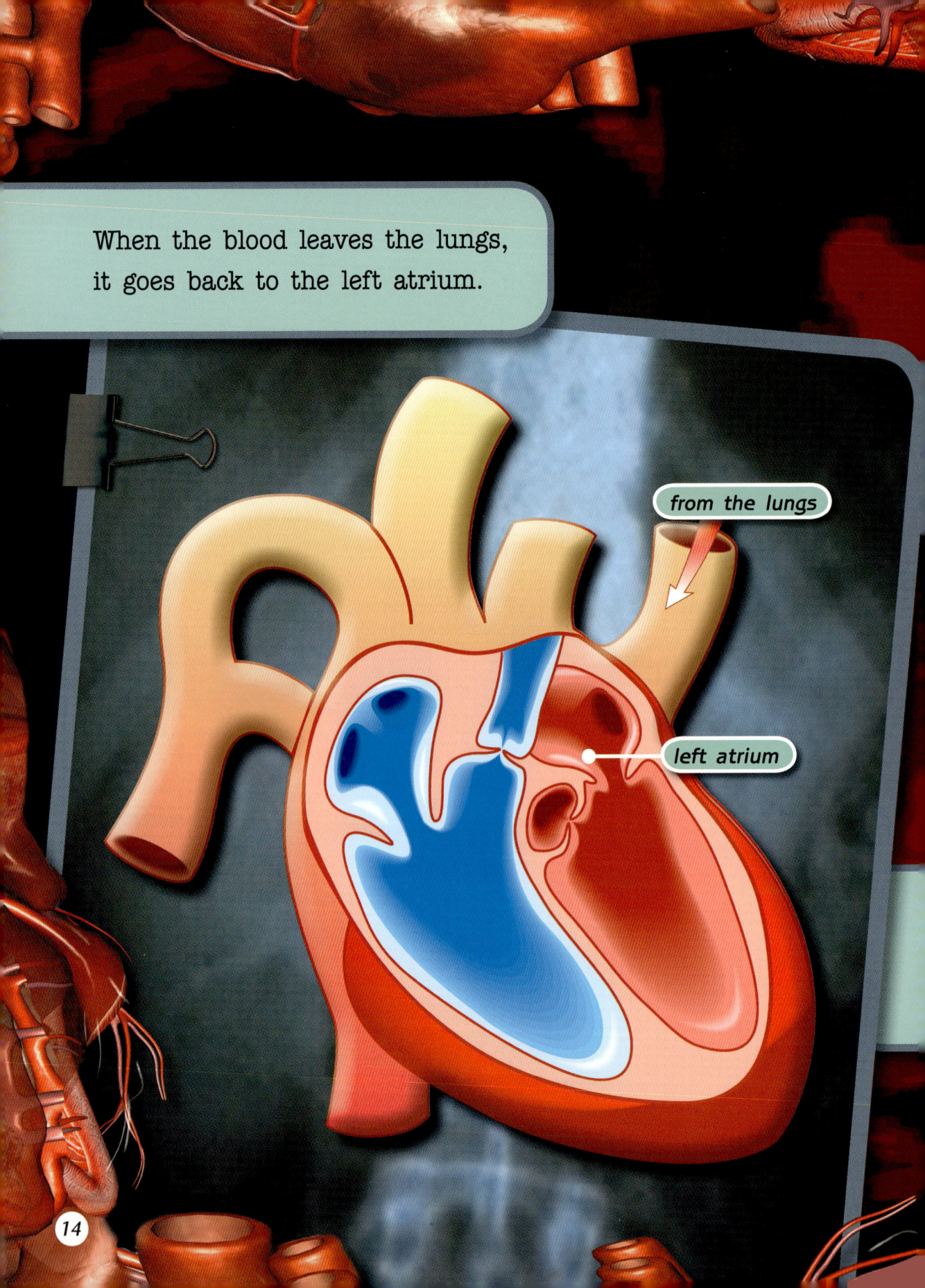

When the blood leaves the lungs, it goes back to the left atrium.

from the lungs

left atrium

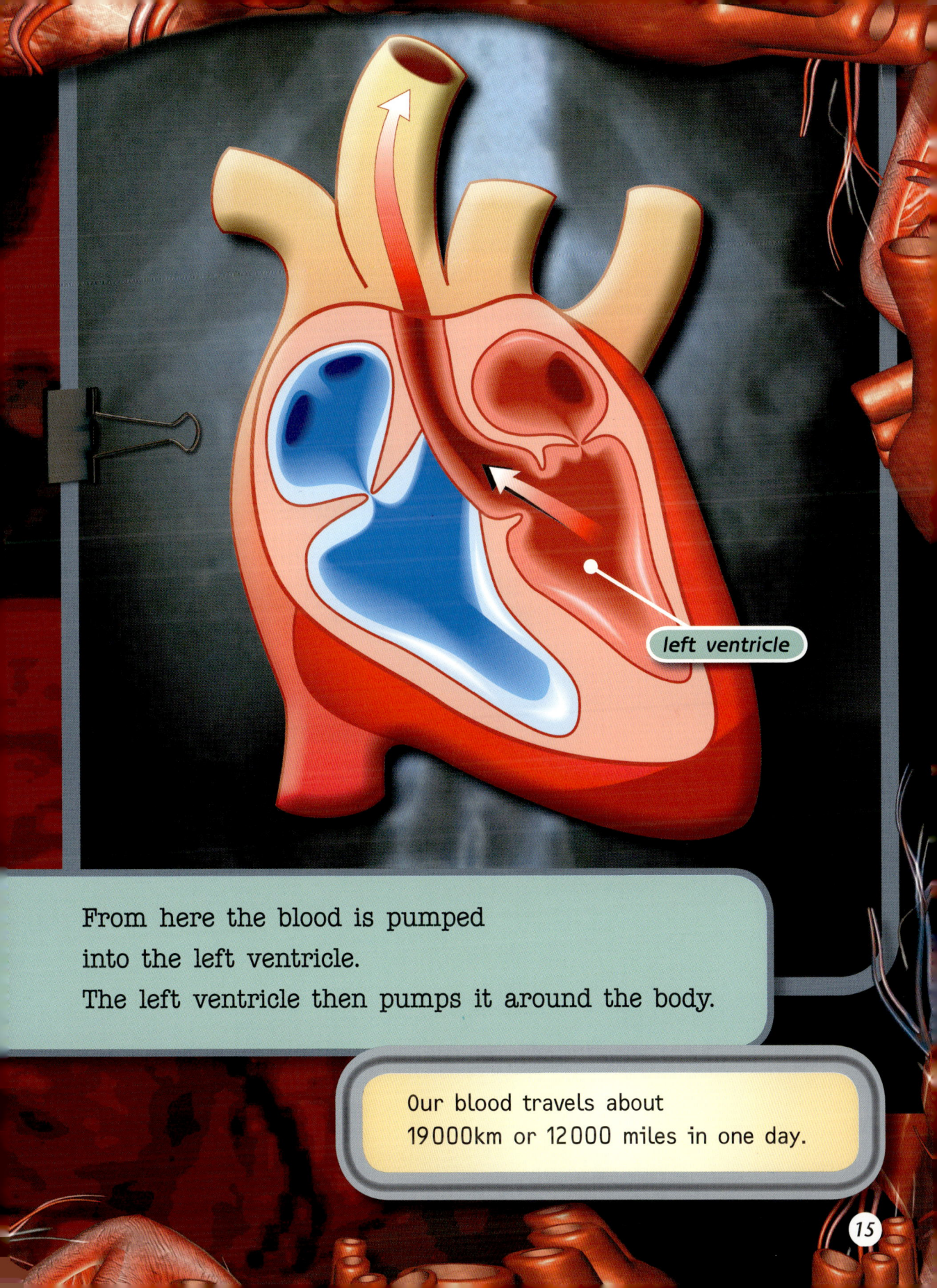

left ventricle

From here the blood is pumped
into the left ventricle.
The left ventricle then pumps it around the body.

Our blood travels about
19 000 km or 12 000 miles in one day.

Chapter 4

THE BEATING HEART

The beating sound of the heart is made by the four valves inside the heart.

A beating sound is made each time a valve closes to stop blood going the wrong way.

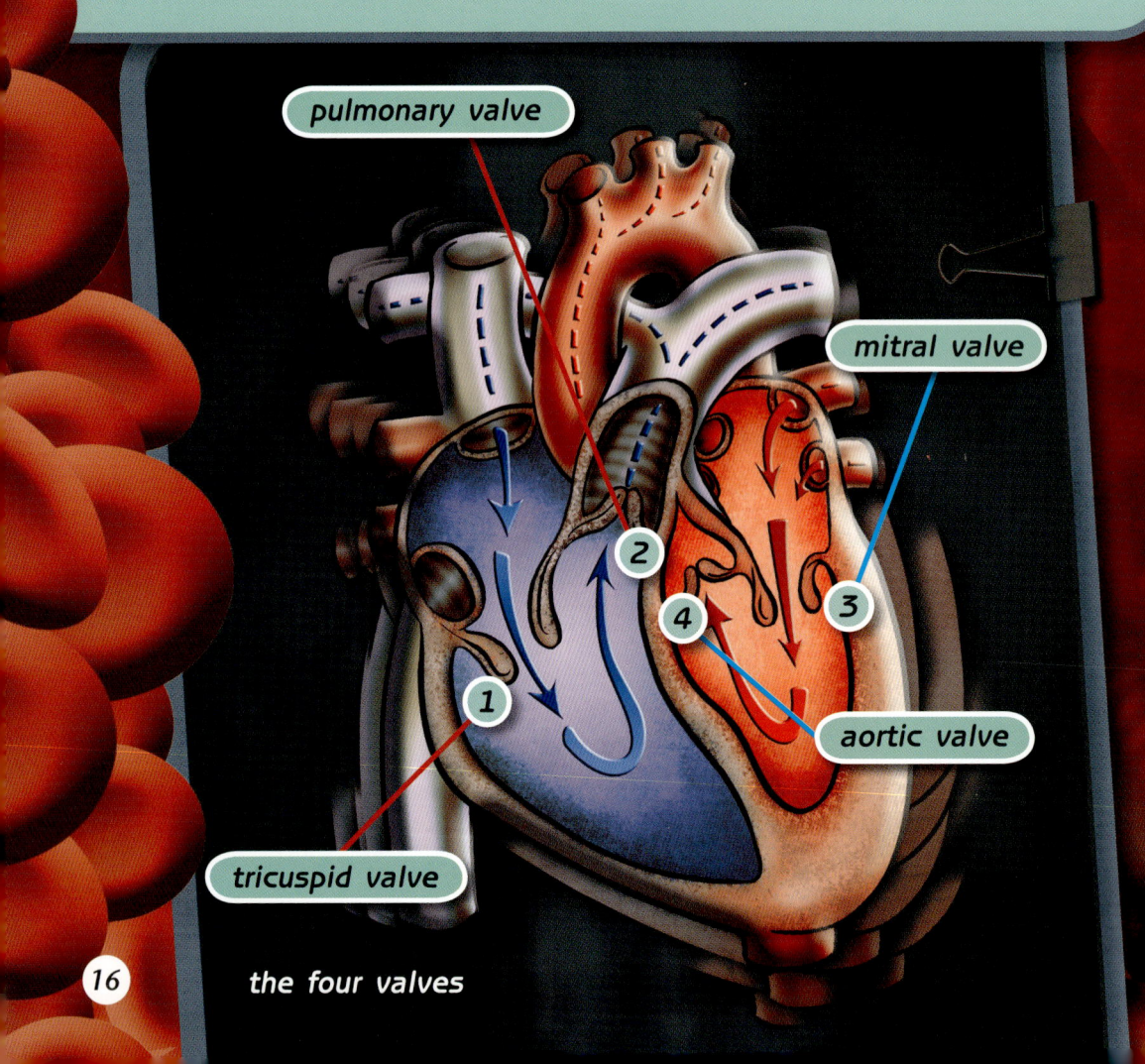

- pulmonary valve
- mitral valve
- aortic valve
- tricuspid valve

the four valves

There are many ways to listen to someone's heart beat.

Before each heart beat, the heart fills with blood, then it pushes the blood out.

The heart does this all day and all night.

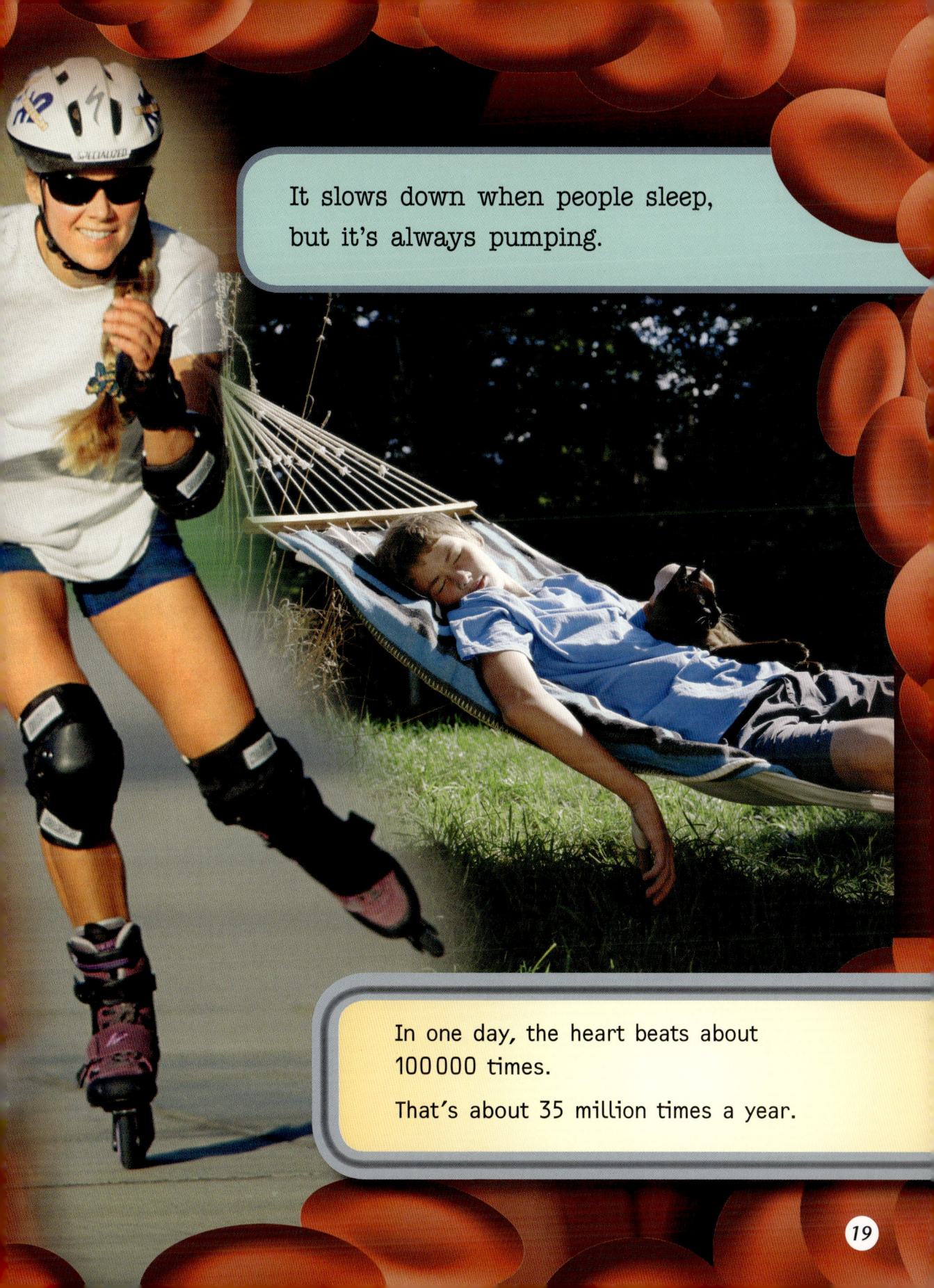

It slows down when people sleep, but it's always pumping.

In one day, the heart beats about 100 000 times.

That's about 35 million times a year.

Chapter 5
THE HEALTHY HEART

A healthy heart can pump oxygen-filled blood around the body.

When the heart isn't healthy, the body doesn't work as well as it should.

The way you move and the food you eat has a lot to do with how well your heart works.

healthy heart = healthy person

Here are three ways to keep the heart healthy:

don't smoke

eat healthy food

get lots of exercise

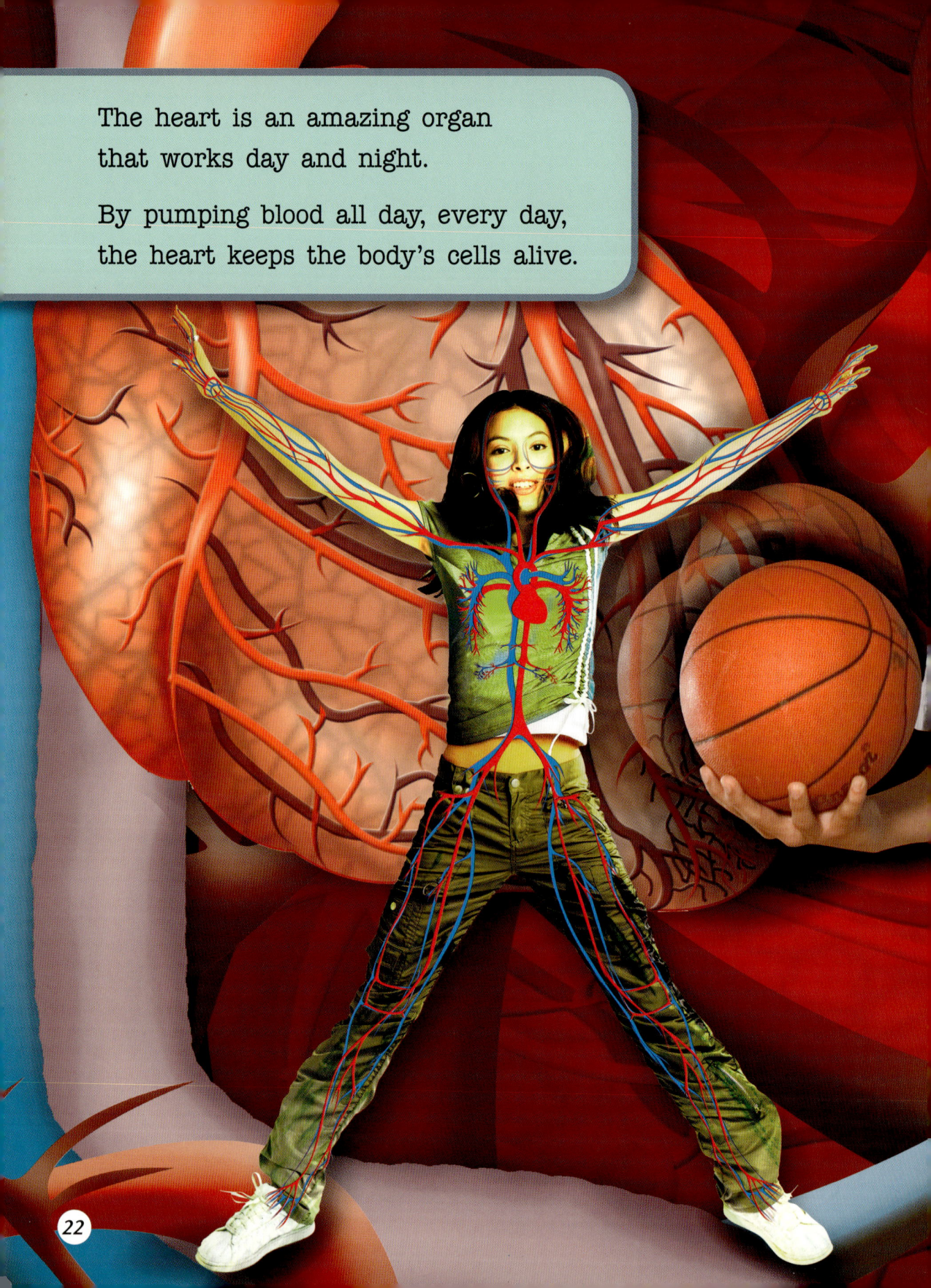

The heart is an amazing organ that works day and night.

By pumping blood all day, every day, the heart keeps the body's cells alive.

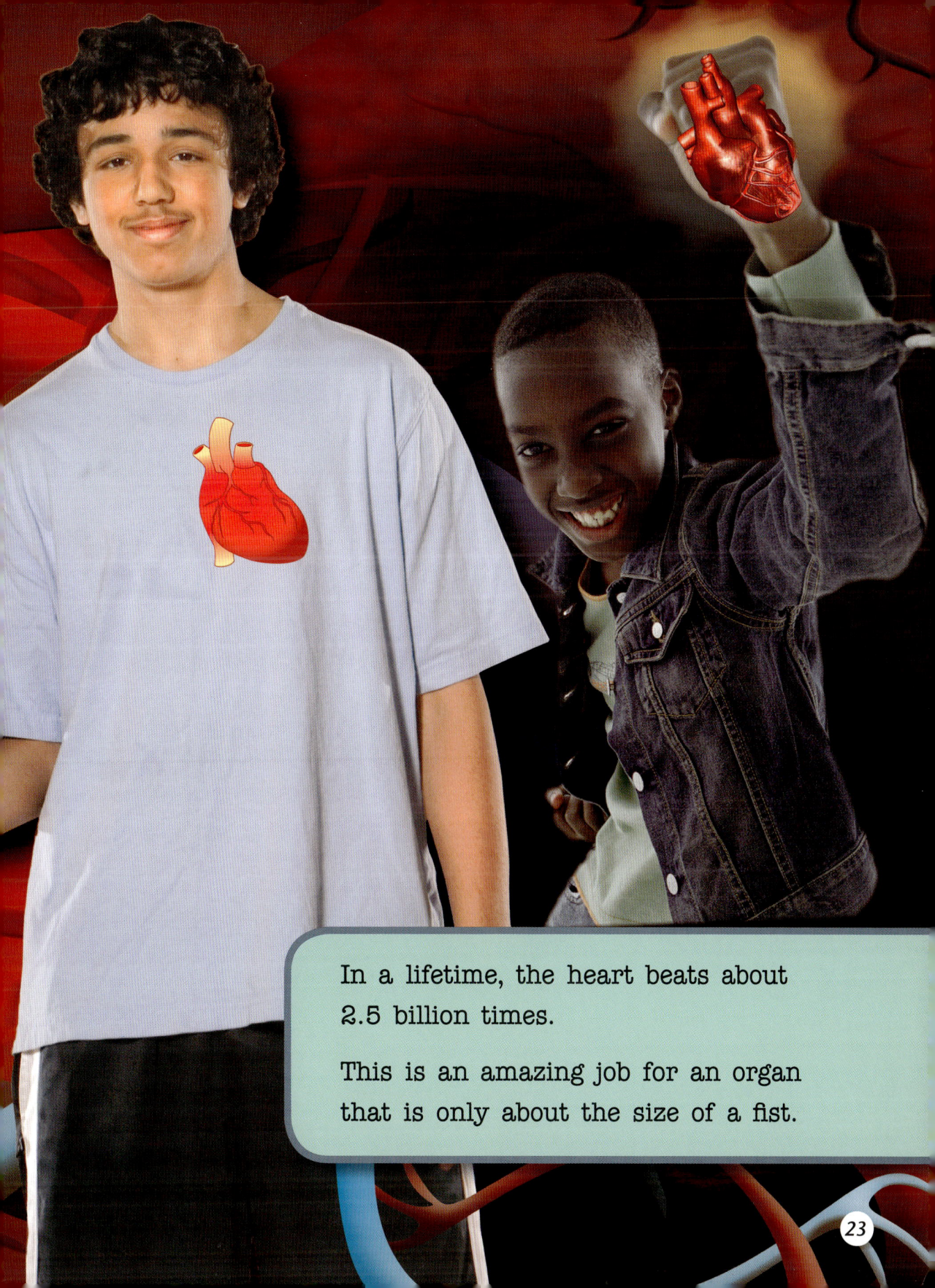

In a lifetime, the heart beats about 2.5 billion times.

This is an amazing job for an organ that is only about the size of a fist.

Glossary

cell   the smallest structural unit of a living thing

organs parts of the body that perform a specific function. The heart, lungs and brain are all organs.

valves openings in an organ or blood vessel that allow blood to flow through in one direction

Index

cell   5, 11, 22

food   11, 21

lungs   13, 14

muscle   4

organs   4, 22, 23

oxygen   11, 13, 20

valves   9, 16